SO MUCH STUFF, SO LITTLE SPACE

Creating and Managing the Learner-Centered Classroom

Susan Nations and Suzi Boyett

Maupin House

So Much Stuff, So Little Space
Creating and Managing the Learner-Centered Classroom

Cover design: Danny Mendoza
Layout design: Maria Messenger
Photographer: Laurie MacDonald

Library of Congress Cataloging-in-Publication Data

Nations, Susan.
  So much stuff, so little space : creating and managing the
  learner-centered classroom / Susan Nations and Suzi Boyett.
    p. cm.
  Includes bibliographical references.
  ISBN 0-929895-52-5 (pbk.)
  1. Classrooms--Planning. 2. Elementary school facilities--
  Planning. 3. Classroom environment. I. Boyett, Suzi,
  1970- II. Title.

LB3325.C5 N38 2002
371.6'21--dc21   2002011642

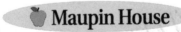

Maupin House Publishing, Inc.
PO Box 90148 • Gainesville, FL 32607
1-800-524-0634 • www.maupinhouse.com

*Publishing Professional Resources
that Improve Classroom Performance*

Contents

Acknowledgements

There are so many people who have been instrumental in helping to shape this book! A sincere thank you goes to our principal, Steve Dragon, who believes deeply in a quality child-centered elementary school environment where teachers can teach and kids can learn. The vision of the administration and staff make Gocio Elementary School a very special place to both of us.

To our friends and colleagues who collaborated with us and shared their thoughts, classrooms and ideas freely and willingly: Judi Blessee, Jamie Boxler, Danielle Brashear, Brenda Bunker, Teresa Campbell, Megan Cawley, Katie Combs, Kathy Corona, Lia Crawford, Steve Crump, Michelle Ford, Heidi Kocur, Ana Perez, Janice Raab, Cheryl Rocco, Cynthia Santacroce, Christine Saunders, Candice SeaceDebra Voege, Sandy Waite, Jamie Ward, and Tymesha Williams. We appreciate you!

A special thank you to our colleagues, Mellissa Alonso and Kristin Boerger for reading the manuscript and giving valuable input.

Thank you to the following students who allowed us to photograph them in various learning environments: Ben Billingsley, Brittany Billingsley, Kyle Blessee, Alisa Herrera, Tyler Manse, Allison Morgan, Adriane Munsey, Andy Munsey, Jordan Nations, and Nathan Ward. Your patience made this a very fun and special project!

We are grateful for our husbands, Ernie Boyett and Don Nations, for giving us time to write, reading the manuscript again and again, and their ongoing support and encouragement. To the Nations' boys (Daniel, Matthew, Jordan, and Aaron), thank you for understanding the time it takes to write a book. We wish to also thank extended families for their enthusiasm and interest in this book.

Foreword

I was truly honored when Suzi Boyett and Susan Nations asked me to write the foreword to their book, *So Much Stuff, So Little Space*. I have the good fortune of interacting with these two consummate educators every day, Suzi as a second-grade teacher and Susan as a literacy resource teacher, grades K–5.

At first I wondered why they chose me to write this foreword, but as I read the book it became quite clear. Two of my emphases as an educator are organization and classroom environment, and their book thoroughly addressed these topics.

Suzi and Susan tell us that "organization is a key to successful teaching." As a former elementary-school teacher for twelve years, and now as a principal, I have found this to be true. Additionally, I have always felt a strong professional concern for the overall classroom environment. Children need a stimulating, orderly, organized environment in which they can find emotional security — a prerequisite, to my way of thinking, for academic achievement.

The authors describe several ways to organize the classroom so that it becomes a comfort zone for all who enter, especially the teacher and students. They point out that this "second home" where students spend as much as one-third of their day must become a safe place where they can feel comfortable taking risks.

Both Suzi and Susan model for others the suggestions and ideas described in this book. One need only visit Suzi's classroom and Susan's workspace to see these well-thought-out and carefully designed practices in action.

This book will prove useful to every teacher, both those for whom organizing comes naturally and those who want to learn how to organize themselves and their classrooms better — a resource for new and seasoned teachers alike. New teachers will scour the pages as they design and create their learning space, and seasoned teachers will find many new ideas for fine-tuning their students' "second home."

Steven E. Dragon
Principal, Gocio Elementary School

Introduction

What are we doing writing a book about organizing a classroom? We have asked ourselves this question many times while putting this book together. Like many teachers, we find ourselves saving materials for that one teachable moment that *might* happen. With budgets tighter than ever, we have learned we need to be our own best resource. Scrounging for materials seems to be an educator's way of life. But, as class sizes increase, and we find ourselves with less space in the classroom, we discover that we need to organize those resources while making the most of our useable space. We have designed this book to help you do just that. Writing this book has also served to reassure us that we can be organized, efficient, and resourceful all at once.

What made you pick up this book? Perhaps you are just starting out a school year and looking for fresh ideas. You might be picking up the book midyear, when you are drowning in piles of paperwork. Regardless of where you are in the organizational process, this book will be a handy tool to help you consider ways to make your classroom environment more user friendly for both you and your students.

Using This Book

If you are at the beginning of a year or starting out in your first classroom, we suggest that you begin reading in Chapters One and Two. If you are a seasoned teacher or are picking this book up midyear, you might want to begin in Chapter Two as you consider ways to make your classroom more homelike.

Each subsequent chapter provides a quick reference for organizing at different points of the school year.

Throughout the book we share vignettes from our own classroom experience. These first-person accounts are labeled with our names, so that you will know who is telling the story.

We understand very well that classroom organization and maintenance is not only hard work but also an ongoing process. We also know that it pays off with more time for teaching, less classroom stress, greater peace of mind for teacher and students, and more effective learning. We hope that on your professional journey, *So Much Stuff* becomes a valuable reference that you pick up again and again.

CHAPTER 1

Starting Out Right

"You never get a second chance to make a first impression," some wise person once said, a maxim we have found especially true as a school year gets underway.

So suppose it's the beginning of a new school year. You wake up from your relatively relaxed summer doings, ready to get back to work, filled with anticipation. But even before your students set foot in your classroom, your optimism can quickly disappear under a blanket of unorganized materials. Does the following scenario sound familiar?

Day One: You arrive at school, eager to get into your classroom to start putting everything in order, but the principal calls an all-day meeting. As you sit there, you doodle ideas for your schedule and your classroom design on the day's agenda. After the meeting, you stay at school late digging out materials you'll need for day two.

Day Two: You head off to school, hopes high: Today you expect to get most of your classroom set up. You spend the morning arranging desks or tables. Around noon, you take a break and spend a long lunch visiting with your colleagues. Back in your room, you feel overwhelmed by all that remains undone. Once again, you stay late, making a list for day three.

Day Three: In your classroom, you rush around shoving piles of materials and paper into cabinets to prepare for today's Parent Open House. You throw together a few bulletin boards to make the room presentable. You quickly make name tags and a sign for the door to welcome your new students. You put on a smile and greet parents and students for an hour. When open house ends, you panic about the next day's lesson plan.

Perhaps you have felt like this at the beginning of a year; maybe you feel like this right now. It is hard not to. The good news is, your first few days don't have to be this way. The rest of this chapter is packed with ideas to get your school year off to a successful start.

We find it helps to think of our classroom each August or September as an artist's empty canvas. It has endless possibilities, and we can design it to fit our needs, at the same time considering what our students will need to be successful. In *How to Be an Effective Teacher: The First Days of School*, classroom management expert Harry K. Wong notes that kids want to know seven things when they come to school on the first day. Table 1 lists those seven things and suggests ways to help answer students' questions.

If the student wants to know...	Then the teacher should...
Am I in the right room?	Post all names on the classroom door at the students' eye level. Stand at the door to greet students as they arrive.
Where am I supposed to sit?	Label desks or tables with student names. Adhere name tags to the desk with clear contact paper.
What are the rules in this classroom?	Post a few simple rules in a prominent place. Plan to introduce and review these several times during the first week.
What will I be doing this year?	Post a daily schedule in a prominent place. Introduce students to some of the thematic units you will be teaching this year. Let older students have a textbook-browsing time during the first week of school.

If the student wants to know...	Then the teacher should...
How will I be graded?	Post the grading scale along with sample work for older students. All students should know and understand what constitutes quality work in your class.
Who is this teacher as a person?	Display family photos or special mementos on your desk. Create a book or poster to introduce yourself to your students.
Will the teacher treat me as a human being?	Stand at the door to greet students as they arrive. Use their names throughout the day. For young students, kneel to their eye level when talking to them.

TABLE 1

While these seven questions are on students' minds the first day of school, they need to be in *our* minds long before students ever arrive. Our goal is to design a classroom where both we and our students can get our work done in a positive and productive manner. We can help by setting up clearly defined spaces, organizing teaching and learning resources, and creating a user-friendly environment before we greet students on the first day of school.

Setting Up Clearly Defined Spaces

Visit any school during the weeks before the students arrive and you are likely to see people dragging furniture from one side of a room to another. The placement of classroom furniture defines learning spaces for students and is one of the most critical decisions we make before classes begin. But instead of just starting to move desks around, we can save a lot of energy by first considering the floor plan of our classroom.

Some classroom layouts present a greater challenge than others. Some lack ample shelves and storage. Others have large physical obstacles to overcome, such as a furnace, a column, or some other permanent fixture. Still others have an odd shape or size. Think about your own classroom. What design challenges will you need to conquer as you set it up for successful learning?

For classrooms of an odd shape or size or with large obstacles, it is worth taking the time to look for another room in the building that is quite similar. By exploring the school, we have many times found the answers to such challenges right next door. We can find out what other teachers are doing to handle their space issues and select a few ideas to try as we set up our own room.

If lack of shelves or storage space is an issue, Chapter Four provides suggestions for ways to organize. A tip: When a product at a grocery store or food mart has sold out, the stores often discard the wire racks or shelves that displayed them. Retailers are usually willing to donate these items to teachers.

After making plans for the shape and size of our classroom, we can consider the furniture arrangement. We can ask ourselves:

- What large group space(s) will I need?
- What small group space(s) will I need?
- How will I arrange for easy movement through the room?
- Is there a place for students to line up when exiting the classroom?
- Does each student have storage space?
- How will I use my walls and bulletin boards?
- Do all students have visual access to the board or overhead?
- Are there spaces for group as well as independent learning?

Have you ever moved all of the furniture in your classroom only to find you didn't like it? We have. Save your back! Before moving a single piece of furniture, arrange a plan on paper.

The illustration below shows an excellent example of a completed classroom map.

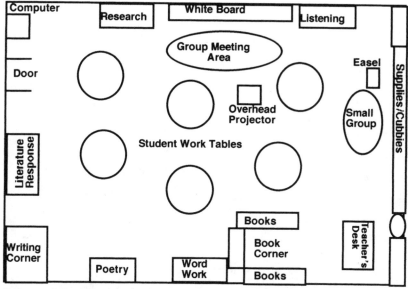

Mrs. Nations' Primary Classroom

Excerpted from: *Primary Literacy Centers: Making Reading and Writing STICK!*
by Susan Nations and Mellissa Alonso, Maupin House Publishing.

Sample classroom map

You will need:

- ✓ 12"x18" (or 12"x12" if your room is more square) sheet of construction paper to represent your classroom
- ✓ Ruler
- ✓ Several sizes of sticky notes
- ✓ Pencil with eraser

1. Draw in any structures and features that cannot be moved (doors, sink, cabinets, shelves, and so on).

2. Use sticky notes to represent movable furniture (student desks, bookcases, file cabinets, small group tables, center tables, etc.).

Teacher rearranging the classroom map

3. Arrange your furniture on the map. Think about proximity issues during this step. For example, an art center will need to be near the sink, and the classroom library may need to be large enough for class meetings.

4. After you are satisfied with the design of your classroom, try moving the furniture to make sure it fits.

Organizing Teaching and Learning Resources

Once we are satisfied with the furniture placement, we can begin thinking about how to organize teacher and student materials, a process which starts with having a comprehensive plan in mind. Table 4, "The First 20 Days of School — Setting Up for Success," provides an outline for daily modeling and teaching of procedures and routines for the beginning of the school year.

We have found it's a good idea to keep resources we will use during the first six weeks easily accessible. Everything else needs to be out of sight (but never out of mind). There's no need to have access to winter themes or decorations in August, for instance, and there is nothing more frustrating than searching for and never finding that one piece of paper that will make the day's lesson a smashing success.

What materials will you need in your classroom for the first six weeks? Pull those items out of summer storage and lay them out. We find it helps to organize materials by theme, subject, or sequence of use. You can store these materials in the files, closets, and shelves in your classroom for easy access. (For more about filing and storage, see Chapter Five.)

It helps to keep instructional materials separated by subject. For example, you can designate a few shelves for math manipulatives, textbooks, and other math-related items. Having such materials available when and where they are needed helps build a positive and effective learning environment.

We suggest that you take all the things you won't need for a while and put them away — or throw them away! If there's not enough room in the classroom, check the rest of the school for possible storage options for anything that you need to keep. If there's not enough room at school, take the materials home or consolidate. We know that throwing anything away poses quite a challenge for teachers. We've all said, "I might use it someday." But realistically, we can gather anything we might need from students or colleagues relatively quickly.

I recently went through some old supply boxes and found 60 baby-food jars that I thought I might use someday. Although it was hard, I threw out all but 12, thinking I could put a request out to parents or colleagues when I needed more. This type of consolidation allowed me to go from a large copy-paper box to a shoebox for storage. —Susan

It helps to designate a central area in the classroom for surplus supplies. During the summer, you can buy extra school supplies when they go on sale. One way to organize these is to place them in labeled containers lined up along counters in the classroom. Second-grade teacher Kathy Corona keeps all her extra supplies in a shoe-storage bag inside her classroom closet door. Students know that when they need more glue, a pencil, or a bandage, they can open the door and get it. Having supplies available for students to access on their own helps them be more self-sufficient.

Time spent teaching and modeling the access and use of all materials in the learning environment during the first few weeks of school pays off. It will help students avoid misusing materials and quickly develop a spirit of independence in your classroom.

Planning User-friendly Bulletin Boards

As we think back on our own elementary-school student days, we realize that teachers created most of the classroom wall displays, and that most were for decorative purposes only. The materials that hung there day after day were often commercially created and did little or nothing to stimulate our learning. While not unfriendly, these bulletin boards did not engage students or encourage them to interact with or use. In today's classrooms, an effective environment is user-friendly and functional, with bulletin boards that both reflect student inquiry and promote independence.

Some teachers prefer to start the year with bare classroom walls. Together with their students, they set them up and decorate them, which makes students partners in the process. If this appeals to you, you can choose a color scheme for your room ahead of time (see Chapter Two) and prepare materials beforehand that you and the students will probably want to use. You can also cover bulletin boards with some background fabric or paper. If you choose this method of set-up, you will still want your classroom to be inviting to your students from the moment they enter. One primary teacher placed yellow construction tape across each bulletin board labeled, "under construction," which made her students eager to be a part of creating the classroom with their new teacher.

Many teachers do not like the thought of beginning the year with bare walls. If you fall into this category, we advise you to go ahead and decorate, but *not to overdo it*. For instance, you could post a few basic items such as classroom rules, students' names, and a calendar before students arrive and still save some decisions for you and your students to make together. You could wait to decide where your class will keep extra supplies, for example, where the fish tank will go, or how to organize the book corner.

Regardless of the approach we choose, it's important to plan how we are going to use bulletin boards. While some decorative or seasonal bulletin boards may fit the bill from time to time, we have found it effective to make functional learner-centered boards part of our classroom. Table 2 gives examples of some boards that work well in classroom set-ups.

Bulletin Board	Type/Function
Calendar Math	Provides daily practice on math-related topics and concepts, such as place value, patterns, money, measurement, graphing, and problem solving.
Literature Response Board	Promotes student inquiry through sentence stems and student's written responses to books. Sentence stems to include: When I read, I feel..., I know..., I like..., I notice..., I remember..., I think..., I wonder....
Student Work Display	Highlights quality work of individual students. Displays may include projects, book reports, science observations, poetry, student writing, etc.
Theme Board	Focuses on current instructional themes in science and social studies. May include research information, key points, specialized vocabulary, inquiry questions, etc.
Word Wall	Lists frequently used words alphabetically. Students determine which words will be posted. Words are often those misspelled in student writing.
Writing	Features student writing, the current target skill(s), and other writing-process information.

TABLE 2

Like any environment, classrooms need to be monitored and freshened up occasionally. Walls and materials filled with print that is unfamiliar to students not only will go unused but also may distract students. We can turn bulletin boards into educational tools if we enlist the help of students early in the year. The boards help them decide what they need to be successful. It's a good idea to remove whatever does not directly relate to your teaching or your students' learning. Less is sometimes more.

Organizing the First Twenty Days: Setting Up for Success

In addition to considering our classroom walls, there are other things we can do to set up a learner-centered environment. We can prepare designated areas where we will later post classroom procedures. Plan to develop your classroom procedures with your students during the first week of school. What will students do when they first enter your room? How do they know when to sharpen a pencil? Where do they go to borrow a marker? (See Table 3 on page 11 for sample procedure boards.)

Procedure Boards and Job Charts

Suzi uses a morning procedure board to help her students ease into their day. The list reminds students what they should do as they enter the room. Table 3 shows several different kinds of sample procedure boards. She also posts a daily agenda on a white board to show her students what she has planned and what she expects of them each day. At a glance, they can see the daily schedule, which also keeps everyone aware of the times for lunch, special classes, and so on. Both of these systems provide a sense of security for students as they learn their new routine.

A classroom job chart provides another way to define procedures. Early in the school year, students can brainstorm a list of possible classroom jobs. The teacher determines how often these jobs will rotate — some teachers rotate them daily; others, weekly or monthly. It often works well to have enough jobs to give each child regular responsibilities. Tymesha

Student checking job board

Sample Procedure Boards

Morning Routine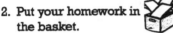

1. Empty your backpack.

2. Put your homework in the basket.

3. Sharpen two pencils.

4. Say "Good Morning" to a friend.

5. Read a book or write in your journal.

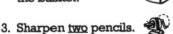

Sharpening Pencil

1. Sharpen two pencils when you arrive in the morning.

2. If your pencils break, raise your hand.

3. Sharpen one pencil. Count to ten while you sharpen.

4. Check to see if the sharpener needs to be emptied.

5. Return to your seat quietly.

Restroom Procedures

1. Raise your hand for permission to go to the restroom.

2. Use the bathroom with care and respect.

3. Clean when you are through.

4. Wash your hands.

5. Return to your seat quietly.

Dismissal Procedures

1. Get your backpack and lunchbox.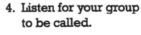

2. Put any papers to go home in your take-home folder.

3. Clean up your work area.

4. Listen for your group to be called.

5. Say "Good Bye" to your friends.

TABLE 3

Williams creates one weekly job for each of her second-grade students, a system that helps them learn important life skills such as cooperation and teamwork.

As a class, students can write job descriptions and illustrate their writing. Add a photograph of each student doing a job, include their writing, and together it can become a job description book. Hanging the book next to the job chart allows students unsure about what their job entails to refer to the book — a step toward independence, as well as a time-saver for the teacher, who won't have to explain everyone's new jobs every week.

Agenda Boards

A daily agenda board is another way to prepare students for the day. You can post an outline of the day's agenda on a white board or overhead to help you and the students anticipate what activity comes

Daily agenda board

next. Again, it pays off to spend time during the first few weeks of school helping students understand what the daily agenda means.

Agenda and procedure boards work with younger children and nonreaders as well as with students who can read. Younger children and nonreaders need pictures to remind them about each activity or procedure, while readers can use written information to outline their day and give them direction.

Giving students a voice and choice in the classroom allows us to set up clear expectations from the start. With classroom space and storage well defined, we can begin the school year with greater ease and peace of mind, on our way to transforming our students into a community of learners.

The First 20 Days of School — Setting Up for Success

Day 1 – After students arrive, hold a class meeting to create rules. Role-play these rules with students. Allow students to illustrate class rules.	**Day 2** – Introduce procedures and routines for classroom materials. Use agenda board to introduce the daily schedule.	**Day 3** – Students choose seating along with teacher input. Discuss how personal storage space (desk or cubbies) should be kept.	**Day 4** – Add any new supplies that students will be using. Review procedures and routines for appropriate use.	**Day 5** – Reflect on week one with students. Record anything that may need to be reorganized to facilitate student learning.
Day 6 – Review rules with students. Discuss possible classroom displays (i.e., bulletin boards, work space, etc.)	**Day 7** – Designate a place for students to return paperwork. Organize and turn in paperwork to the office. Use clips or large envelopes to store forms.	**Day 8** – Adjust seating if necessary. By now, you will know who can sit in which groups. Continue design of bulletin boards and student work space.	**Day 9** – Revisit classroom materials management. Take time to have students check personal space for organization.	**Day 10** – Decide if your furniture needs to be moved. This may be the time to rearrange desks or shelves to facilitate movement.
Day 11 – Together with your students determine class jobs. Begin making labels for bins and shelves.	**Day 12** – Practice class jobs. Role-play with students. Look around your room. Is it inviting to visitors? What can you do to make it so?	**Day 13** – Begin organizing for small group instruction. Conduct individual assessments to determine placement of students.	**Day 14** – Review procedures and routines. Have students discuss what is going well, and what still needs work. Make a work plan.	**Day 15** – Organize student desks and cubbies. Clean up any piles that have accumulated around your work space.
Day 16 – Clean your desk. Set up student work files or portfolios. Return any papers to students and file the others.	**Day 17** – Rearrange your teacher materials if necessary. Make a list of materials you will need for upcoming units/themes.	**Day 18** – Follow-up on paperwork that needs to be returned to the office. Focus on any last minute assessments for small group placement.	**Day 19** – If necessary, reorganize small materials. Be sure all storage bins and shelves are labeled to create a space for everything.	**Day 20** – Reflect on first month of school with students. Make a list of any changes that need to be made.

CHAPTER 2

Creating a Homelike Environment

As we remember the many classrooms we have visited over the years, some seemed to call out to all who passed by, "Come in and spend time here!" and "This is a true learning place!" Other classrooms seemed to warn, "Run! Don't come in here!" Classrooms that turn away the visitor feel cluttered and stifling. The inviting classrooms are predictable, orderly, and neat, but not sterile. Note that we didn't say they are never messy. In fact, we find that places where engaged learning takes place are often messy, yet easy to clean up because there is a place for everything. They are, in fact, homelike.

In *Integrated Thematic Instruction*, author and educational consultant Susan Kovalik writes: "The room speaks for you. Just as our homes get their most thorough cleaning when company is coming, the classroom must be inviting — clean, yet not institutionally bare, rich without being cluttered, focused without being sterile." Giving students a sense of home when they are in our classrooms fosters trust in us as their teachers and bolsters their confidence for learning.

The remainder of this chapter focuses on the four characteristics that we believe are typical of the ideal "homelike" classroom. A homelike classroom environment is:

- Calm and predictable
- Safe and comfortable
- Structured and dependable
- Orderly and reliable

Making the Classroom Calm and Comfortable

When I first began teaching at a small school in Indiana, there was an emphasis on making the classrooms more calming and homelike. Teachers were encouraged to choose two or three complementary colors and use those colors when decorating bulletin boards and other classroom spaces. We bought items like containers, pillows, and lamps to match the color scheme. When I moved to Florida, people would often comment on how warm and "homey" my room was. While they never said exactly what it was that made them feel that way, I am sure that it was the predictability of the color scheme and other homelike touches that contributed to their impression. —Suzi

When we decorate a room at home, often we choose a few colors and stick with that color plan when we buy furniture and accessories. When we decorate our classrooms, we can follow the same basic rules. We may find that we already favor certain colors in our classrooms. If they complement each other, why not use these colors to decorate? We can use them when choosing storage bins, containers, bulletin board backgrounds, and other accessories. Sticking to two or three colors keeps a classroom — or anywhere else — from becoming overstimulating. The result is pleasing to the eye and inviting to all who enter.

Elementary teacher Cynthia Santacroce likes sunflowers. When she picked her classroom colors, she chose yellow and green. She made curtains with a fabric that had a sunflower design and found some inexpensive sunflower rugs to add to the decor. Her students noticed these touches immediately, and both they and Cynthia found her classroom a warm and inviting place. Some teachers may want to choose colors that reflect an instructional theme. If your theme involves many earth concepts, for example, you might choose greens, blues, or browns. If your theme revolves around the United States, you could think about red, white, and blue.

Having a basic color scheme can save time and money. You'll save time when bulletin boards need changing because you will need to change only what's on the boards, not the paper and border. As other teachers in the building settle on their own colors or change their color schemes, you may be able to save money by trading materials and accessories.

The Comforts of Home

Many teachers like to bring homelike furniture and decorative items into their classrooms. For example, Katie Combs has two small couches in her third-grade classroom that she covers in quilts to make a cozy reading and learning nook. Kindergarten teacher Janice Raab set a cardboard fireplace she bought during the holidays into a classroom corner, which she calls "Fireside Reading." Students enjoy curling up by the "fire" with their books. Christine Saunders uses lamps and plants to make a homelike setting for the rocking chair in her kindergarten classroom.

Music

Soft music creates a calming environment for students. Many teachers play selections when students are working; research suggests that classical music stimulates the brain. Mellissa Alonso uses both classical and natural-sounds music when her third-graders are in writing workshop. She finds that the music provides a relaxing, stress-free atmosphere that helps students focus and concentrate on the tasks at hand. "It sets the tone for the classroom," Mellissa says, "and helps us keep our voices low enough so we don't disturb other writers at work."

Fragrances

For the same reason that many people scent their homes with aromatic potpourris, you might consider adding fragrances to

A checklist of ideas to consider for making your classroom more comfortable and homelike:

- Choose two or three complementary colors to use in your room.
- Make it easy for students to find and use materials.
- Accent and decorate with plants.
- Define spaces with a few throw rugs or carpets.
- Provide lamps to make cozy nooks for learning and exploring.
- Hang curtains or valances on windows and over unsightly shelves.
- Place pillows in your classroom library and in other quiet corners.
- Add a couch or comfortable chairs for special reading times.
- Use appealing fragrances throughout the classroom.
- Play soothing music during quiet work times.
- Identify and create a thematic curriculum to provide predictability.

your classroom — to appeal to the senses, to mask unpleasant odors, and to add a pleasing, distinctive character to the room. Sandy Waite uses plug-in fragrances in her intermediate classroom to disguise unwanted odors. The clean fresh-smelling scent is inviting and appealing to visitors as well as to the children. Although floral fragrances that may disturb children with respiratory problems need to be avoided, we have found that citrus, cinnamon, apple, and vanilla work well.

Making the Classroom Safe and Predictable

People enjoy routine. Many of us sit in the same area at meetings, drive the same way to work every day, always brush our teeth before we get dressed. Routines help us feel secure and in charge; they make life more predictable. At the same time, a classroom, like a home, should be a safe haven where we are free to try new things and take risks. Children thrive in a classroom that combines safe, predictable routines that support learning with the encouragement to take risks as they explore new possibilities and skills. Making the environment predictable is one way to ensure a sense of safety for students.

A Morning Routine

When students enter your classroom in the morning, what is the first thing they do? To make sure that this is never in question, students need to know the morning routine early in the school year. (See Chapter One, page 11.)

In my first-grade classroom, this was the students' morning routine:

1. Empty your backpack.
2. Put your homework in the basket.
3. Sharpen two pencils.
4. Say "Good morning" to someone.
5. Read a book or write in your journal.

I spent time during the first few weeks of school introducing and practicing each step. Once students understood the routine, they were independent and could focus on the day ahead of them. The predictability meant that I could have conversations with individual students as they entered the room. I didn't have to worry that the other students would not know exactly what to do. —Susan

A morning routine helps students feel safe, and early in the year, such a routine helps them adjust to their new "home," their classroom. They know they can count on it. As you picture your own classroom, ask yourself how your students enter. Is it with an "I know what to do and I'm ready to conquer the day" attitude? Or is it in a state of mild confusion? If they are often confused, it may mean that the classroom is not yet an entirely safe haven for them. After all, it's hard to feel safe when you're confused. Students spend up to one-third of their day with you. If you want to make sure that they feel safe to learn in your classroom, you have the tools to accomplish it.

Making the Classroom Well-Supplied and Useable

Imagine that you're at home ready to start on an exciting project. You have all of the materials you need, but where are the needle-nosed pliers and the flat-head screwdriver (or the baking pan and measuring cups, or the spade and gardening gloves)? Like any other activity, learning is easier if you have the tools in hand to do the job right. Knowing where to find the materials we need and trusting that they will be available when we need them is critical to productivity. If we have to go in search of materials and tools, we not only waste time but also may lose interest in the project entirely. A well-supplied, organized classroom helps students be more productive during their work time.

It works best to keep materials in a central location where students have easy access to them. In most homes, children do not have to ask where paper and writing materials are. They simply go and get them whenever they want or need them. This is the same behavior and sense of self-sufficiency we want to encourage in the classroom. In the end, it provides a less stressful environment for the teacher, too.

In my classroom, I always wanted to make my supplies accessible to students at all times. It wasn't until my sixth year that I figured out how to do this. Labeled crates and baskets along a counter contain supplies for students to use as needed. —Suzi

We have found it important to discuss with our students when it is appropriate for them to go and get supplies and how they need to use and care for each supply basket. "How will I ever keep my students from hoarding these supplies?" you may ask. You can teach them to get only what they need and assure them that the supplies will not run out. They also need to know that if they find any of these materials on the floor or elsewhere in the classroom, they are responsible for returning them to their proper crate or basket. This almost makes the supplies regenerate themselves. They also need to understand that their access to supplies depends on their taking care of them and using them appropriately. Misuse will eventually result in loss of access.

Depending on grade level, different supplies will be more or less appropriate for students to get for themselves. For example, upper graders may need rubber bands, while primary students probably do not. Some supplies that you might consider keeping available to students are the following:

Band-Aids. Young children often need Band-Aids for little cuts and scrapes. (Some children even need them for "boo-boos" that no one else can see.) We include Band-Aids on our student supply list at the beginning of the year. It is much easier to leave them accessible for students to get as needed than to worry about doling them out.

Crayons and markers. Students know that when they lose or misplace a particular color they can go to the basket and replace it immediately.

Glue and glue sticks. Because glue has a tendency to spill inside student desks, it is best to store it upright in a central location.

Paper. Students need paper of all shapes and sizes available during their independent work or center time.

Stapler and staples. Students like having access to these grown-up tools. Supplies last longer if you model how to use only one or two staples to attach pages.

Tape. Useful for repairing torn papers, tape is another supply whose use needs modeling. Teach students how to pull off only a small piece of tape at a time.

Making the Classroom Orderly and Reliable

In an ideal home, we trust that the environment will stay the same. Our furniture and books and TV will stay where they are unless we decide to move them. We can create this same sense of order and reliability in the classroom as well. We have all been in uncomfortable and unproductive places where chaos abounds. Because a chaotic classroom can cause students to lose their focus and become disruptive, establishing an orderly, reliable environment needs to be a priority. In Chapter One we discussed setting up the classroom with a sense of orderliness in mind. Furniture placement and classroom displays set the tone and help establish order in the classroom from day one — it becomes a safe space. Maintaining order in the environment throughout the year fosters a sense of trust among students. They know they have a place they can rely on.

Furniture Placement

In your classroom, you make the early decisions about where you want the furniture. Sometime during the year, you may want to rearrange it. Many well-meaning teachers wait to do any rearranging until after students have left for the day. The next morning, as students arrive, they may get overexcited about the changes; confusion may ensue. Students can take quite a long time to settle into the unexpected new arrangement.

We suggest avoiding possible chaos by making students part of the process. You could discuss with them your ideas for moving desks and other furniture and share your reasoning. If you choose to use the furniture placement plan shown on page 5 with your students, they can manipulate the pieces on the map and help redesign their classroom. This type of shared decision making, which gives students time to adjust to the coming changes ahead of time and gives them some responsibility for the process, gives them a stake in maintaining a safe, reliable, and orderly environment.

Classroom Displays

We are continually amazed at the difference that displays on walls and bulletin boards can make in a classroom. In some classrooms, the bulletin boards still welcome kids to school after they've been there for eight weeks. In others, something new shows up on the boards almost every day.

I found bulletin boards to be a chore in my classroom. I decided to assign one or two students to determine what would go on each board and to monitor it for frayed or torn papers. The students let me know when it was time for a change and helped keep it looking fresh each day. Other students eventually began asking if their work could be displayed on the appropriate boards. I felt almost totally removed from the task of monitoring and updating bulletin boards as the children took more and more responsibility for this important part of our classroom environment. —Susan

Shelley Harwayne, founding principal of the Manhattan New School, has found that

> bulletin boards are not mere white noise. They sound a clarion call, announcing what is valued to all who enter the school. There are good reasons for eliminating all frayed, mediocre, or outdated presentations on schoolhouse walls. We can't talk to students about their work habits when we don't model our own attention to high-quality work.

If I can pass by a bulletin board without stopping to read it or drag someone over to appreciate it, the display is simply not good enough. If designed thoughtfully, bulletin boards can provide a significant way for educators, administrators, and teachers to help parents, visitors, student teachers, volunteers, and students understand the power of the work we do and why we do it.

In our experience, classroom displays reflect what is going on in a classroom. Including students in the selection of material to be displayed not only relieves the teacher of some of the burden of responsibility but also gives students ownership of and pride in the displays. It's all part of a more orderly and reliable — and interesting — classroom environment.

Encouraging Learning

Creating an environment where all children can learn to their fullest potential is the goal of every teacher we know. With class sizes on the rise, and with more students trying to learn in comparatively less space, a classroom well organized and free of clutter is a boon to both students and teachers. We all appreciate reliable and stable environments. To become a "home away from home," our classroom needs to be a familiar, comfortable place to learn.

Many of our students come from home environments where they feel safe and secure. Some others, however, do not. For those students especially, it is important that we create — and involve them in creating — an environment conducive to active, engaged learning. Brain research indicates that children must feel a sense of security and the absence of any real or perceived threat for maximum learning. As teachers, we have taken on a great responsibility: setting up a safe, orderly

A warm, inviting classroom

classroom and creating a homelike environment where every child can learn every day. As Susan Kovalik (1994) suggests, "If you fail at this, nothing else matters."

CHAPTER 3

Regrouping at Midyear and Beyond

It's the middle of the year, and your room is a minor disaster area of ungraded papers, left-behind projects, bookshelves in disarray, and a general excess of *stuff*. You and your students may have hit a midyear slump. Are they still keeping their personal spaces organized? Are they taking care of classroom materials? Are they doing their classroom jobs? If, like many of us, they are victims of the winter blahs, it may be time for a class meeting.

Holding a Class Meeting

One intermediate teacher we know takes her students on a midyear tour around the room. As they walk, they talk about what the expectation is for each space. Then two or more students volunteer to bring the space "up to code."

You too may decide to spend time with your students identifying problem areas in your classroom. One approach is to make a Problem/Solution list on chart paper or the board like the one we've included next in Table 5. Pairs or individuals who volunteer to take charge of the reorganization or clean up the identified areas will be the class's "area experts" or "area monitors," or some other responsible title. Taking the time to reorganize when classroom disorder is adding to your stress level not only gives you some peace of mind but also increases student responsibility for the classroom. It's also a good time for you to focus on and clear out areas that you maintain.

Problem	Solution	Monitor(s)
Computer area is cluttered. Disks are not in order in the box.	Place a mini-garbage can on the table to throw away papers. Put disks in the box in ABC order.	Jordan and Ernie will check the table each day at the end of centers.
Library books are thrown back on shelves.	Place a colored dot on each book that matches a dot on its basket.	Nick and Jessica will check the library in the morning and again before going home.
Marker lids are not on the markers.	Put a sign on the marker basket to remind everyone to "listen for the click."	Carrsyn and Aaron will check each day to make sure markers are put away the right way.

TABLE 5

For one primary teacher, the classroom library presents a real problem. She repeatedly finds books shoved back on the shelves haphazardly, and she lacks the time or patience to straighten it up every day herself. One morning it dawned on her that some of her five- and six-year-olds have gifts of organization. She enlisted their help to check the library each day. These "media clerks" became an important part of the classroom. They were able to take care of the library at times when she had small groups. Children often relied on the media clerks to help them return books to the proper place. The classroom library quickly became both more organized and more inviting.

Attacking Key Clutter Areas

In January or February we have often found ourselves saying, "Next year I'll do this differently," or "I'll be more organized next August." Why this tendency to view the rest of this year as a lost cause? Why wait? We know why, of course. The task — whatever it is — feels too overwhelming. Who wants to tackle a huge reorganization project while also filling out report cards, planning daily instruction, and managing ongoing assessments? Things aren't that bad; we need to use our energy for what's on our plate *right now*; we'd rather just limp along until the end of the year and start over in the fall.

What's so hard to remember is how good it feels to be organized, how much extra time and energy it actually *gives* us, and how it eases so many stresses and problems.

Where does clutter accumulate in your classroom? Most elementary-school teachers have one or two key areas that cause them headaches. Now is the time to renew those promises you made to yourself in August or September. So you won't even have to think about how to do this (you can just get right to work!), we've listed typical trouble spots, along with specific organizing tasks in each that often cry out to be done.

Classroom Meeting Space

Discard any charts that you are no longer using. Return Big Books and read-aloud books to their proper places. Throw away dry-erase markers, chalk, and other writing utensils that no longer work. Restock materials you use regularly in this area such as sentence strips, chart paper, markers, pointers, and so on.

Counters

Completely clear counter tops to wash them and reorganize. Remove any items you or your students will not be using. Put away all materials from themes that you have already taught. File or return student papers. Throw away anything that is outdated or that has not been used during the first half of the year.

Pet Areas

Designate students who will maintain pet areas. Clearly label and store food and other supplies in small plastic containers close to the pet cage. For cages that have bedding, keep a small duster or hand broom and dustpan available to clean up spills around the cage area.

Sink Area

Throw away any paintbrushes or paints that are not useable. Consider purchasing new paints. Check glue bottles to find out which ones still work. Consolidate partial bottles of glue to create more space. Put away anything that you are no longer using.

Storage Closet

Do you need more containers to organize your teaching materials? Midyear is a great time to find them, because stores often discount their organizers at this time of year. Check to make sure your bins and shelves are clearly labeled. Store similar items together. Dig all the way to the back and throw away everything you will not need.

Mid-year clutter

Your Desk

Sort papers into three piles: file, return to students, and throw away. Elementary-school principal Steve Dragon puts all papers that will need his attention in a paper tray, anchored with a large blue paperweight. He knows that he needs to check the tray regularly to sort, file, or discard papers. Putting all papers in one space eliminates that frantic search for a missing paper. It not only saves time, but your space looks more organized, and so do you.

Technology Areas

Keep disposable dustcloths in this area for cleaning computer screens and keyboards. Store all CDs and floppy disks in a file basket alphabetically by subject area. Many times computer areas are nests of cords and wires. Use bread ties or rubber bands to wrap excess cords and keep the plug area safe and tidy.

Top of File Cabinets

File all papers and original copies in appropriate places. If you can, file as you go rather than piling papers on top of the cabinet. If this is beyond you, designate one day each month to be your "file day," and write this date into your daily plans. Remove all other items not needed from the top of the file cabinet. Consider placing a plant on top of the file cabinet to discourage storing papers there.

Sprucing Up Midyear

Old habits die hard — and so do old bulletin boards and tired routines. Everyone can use a lift after the holidays: it's the perfect time to refresh your classroom for both you and your students.

Daily Routine

My second-grade students come into the classroom each day and have a morning assignment to complete. Beginning midyear, I like to refresh this routine. For example, my students will begin signing in and recording their time of arrival using digital and analog clocks. Eventually, I will remove the digital clock. This goes along with our unit on telling time. It gives them meaningful daily practice on this important skill. Later on, I might choose a different skill focus for them to use during their morning sign-in. —Suzi

Table 6 on the following page suggests some ways to think about refreshing daily classroom routines.

What's the routine?	How can I make it fresh and engaging for students?
Attendance	If you currently call each student's name, consider providing a sign-in sheet or bulletin board. Write a question over the sign-in and let them answer it by signing under the correct answer. For older students, give them the task of taking your attendance. Make this a job that rotates with other classroom tasks.
Lunch count/order	Help young children make their lunch order by signing in under their selected menu. Designate a bulletin board area where students can put their name under the day's menu.
Transitions to other locations at school	Consider taking a different route to specials classes. Encourage students to think of a new way to walk.
Clean up at the end of the day	Play music during clean-up time. Place a checklist on the board for students to follow as they tidy up their personal space.
Handing in and returning student work	Give each student a mailbox or paper tray. Designate one or two students to take charge of returning graded papers.

TABLE 6

I was always amazed at how my students responded to normal everyday tasks when I added a new tool to use. For example, I might give them a highlighter to use instead of asking them to circle something. This small change helped refresh familiar routines for the students. —Susan

Small changes in daily routine can reduce boredom. In our experience, students enjoy even simple modifications and often will approach classroom tasks with new zeal.

Classroom Walls

Is it time to bring some life back to the displays around your classroom walls? Try this "CPR" exercise.

C: Consider and create relevance and usefulness.
Did you and your students create what is displayed?
Do you use it or refer to it regularly?

P: Plan and prepare new materials.
What are your current instructional themes?
What materials would you need to create new displays?

R: Remove and revise outdated, tattered, and faded displays.
Can you revive a display with a new border or background?
Which displays will you remove completely?

We believe that our classrooms, and our classroom wall displays, send a strong message about our values and beliefs about teaching and learning, life in general, and our students. They are often more influential than we realize. If the idea of sprucing up every classroom wall is overwhelming (which it probably is), we suggest choosing one area where you will focus. Don't forget the advantages of involving students in this process! When you are comfortable with that area, begin to focus on another. Eventually, the entire classroom will feel fresh with new possibility.

Even without an entire classroom overhaul, a few simple changes can make a big difference. We've included an ABCs checklist to help as you focus on your midyear reorganization.

The ABCs of Midyear Organization

- ❏ **A**ccept the midyear challenge to reorganize.
- ❏ **B**anish outdated and unused materials.
- ❏ **C**onsolidate manipulatives into tubs and bins.
- ❏ **D**ust bookshelves, counters, and cabinets.
- ❏ **E**liminate old student work and clutter.
- ❏ **F**reshen up your room with a few new homelike touches.
- ❏ **G**ather materials for your next theme.
- ❏ **H**ide away materials from old themes.
- ❏ **I**nspect student work areas.
  (Do you need to replace any supplies?)
- ❏ **J**udge your wall displays. (Are they relevant?)
- ❏ **K**eep an eye on student desks for organization.
- ❏ **L**ocate resources needed to teach your next theme.
- ❏ **M**inimize key clutter areas.
- ❏ **N**egotiate changes with students
  (schedule, procedures, care of classroom).
- ❏ **O**rganize your desk.
- ❏ **P**lace original copies of worksheets in files.
- ❏ **Q**uestion yourself. What stuff do you *really* need?
- ❏ **R**esolve to maintain an organized environment for the remainder of the year.
- ❏ **S**ort classroom library books into labeled bins or shelves.
- ❏ **T**idy classroom meeting space.
- ❏ **U**nite small items in a central location
  (paper clips, tacks, rubber bands, etc.).
- ❏ **V**erify and update student information.
- ❏ **W**ash countertops and student desk tops.
- ❏ e**X**amine your daily routines and procedures.
- ❏ **Y**ak with colleagues and share ideas.
- ❏ **Z**one learning spaces in your room.

An Organized, Learner-Centered Classroom

The following photographs will take you on a 360 degree presentation of an organized, learner-centered classroom. The sequence begins at the door of the room and continues around at approximately 45 degree turns per picture. A book cannot provide complete sensory stimulation so please note that this primary classroom uses yellows and greens as complimentary colors. Soft music plays in the background and the room smells clean and fresh from a fragrance spray. Some natural light is seen through a window in the corner of the room. You will notice highlighted features in this classroom that are discussed throughout this book.

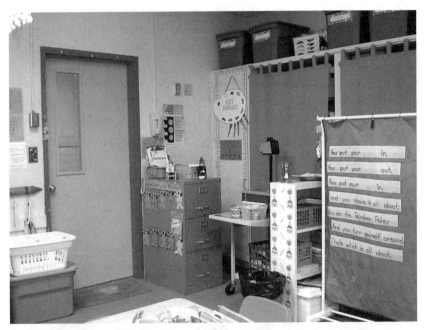

A curtain used to hide storage areas and an interactive pocket chart

A student word wall at eye level, a well-organized writing center, and charts created by the teacher with help from students

A literacy-rich environment with a guided reading table and a class meeting area

Poetry that is easily accessible for students, attractive rugs, and kid-sized furniture

A user-friendly bulletin board and accessible student supplies

A well-organized teacher space and student cubbies

Literacy tubs and student mailboxes

CHAPTER 4

Reorganizing at Any Time

No matter how organized we are, odd piles of papers and materials accumulate, supplies and cubbies and desks get less than orderly, and we have to remind ourselves with some sternness that we *want* to be organized. Organization is a key to successful teaching, and it is an ongoing process. We welcome the days when we clean it all at once; more often, we try to do a little each day.

One of the big secrets to getting and staying organized is to have a place for everything. We've collected the following suggestions to help you organize common classroom materials that contribute to clutter.

Artist's portfolio. Store large charts and posters in a zippered artist's portfolio. This makes them portable and keeps them from getting wrinkled.

Baskets, tubs, or plastic organizer drawers. Use these throughout the classroom to organize books, manipulatives, or papers. Label each shelf or bin clearly so everyone knows what belongs in it.

Chair pockets

Chair pockets. Many teachers in primary grades are trading traditional desks for tables and chairs to promote cooperation and group work. Chair pockets are both personal and portable. They encourage children to stay more organized and they hold less "stuff."

Clothes-drying rack. Use a wooden clothes-drying rack to display your Big Books. Books can be stored over each of the rungs. Students can easily see the titles to make their selections.

Clothespins. Hot-glue clothespins to cabinet doors or walls to display student work. To make these more attractive, cover the tip of the clothespin with a die-cut shape labeled with the student's name. These can be removed with a dull razor blade or by a gentle pull.

Copy-paper boxes or large plastic bins. Store larger or theme-related items in these boxes. Label each box or container clearly. You can stow them away in a large cabinet or a high shelf. If they are visible, consider "hiding" them behind a curtain or covering them in coordinated contact paper. Intermediate teacher Lia Crawford acquired a number of sturdy tomato boxes from a local delicatessen, painted them all the same color, and labeled them to identify contents.

Divided food-serving trays. Susan uses trapezoid tables in her first-grade classroom. She placed one divided serving tray in the middle with a plastic cup in each of the six sections. Students stored their crayons, scissors, and pencils in these cups. They had easy access to them, and they knew exactly where to put things away when they were finished.

File cabinets. Minimize your file-drawer contents by keeping no more than two copies of each worksheet. First-grade teacher Danielle Brashear organizes her hanging files by thematic units. She places all teacher resources, including read-aloud books, art projects, and other theme-related materials for instruction, in a file labeled with the thematic unit. When she begins a new unit, everything she needs is right there.

Fishing tackle boxes, embroidery floss organizers, and toy-car containers. Use these to hold magnetic letters or office supplies. Kindergarten teacher Kristin Boerger uses a drawer organizer in her writing center to store rubber alphabet stamps.

Using a fishing tackle box to store letters

Gift bags. Fill these easily portable bags with theme-related activities to create centers-on-the-go. For storage, consider hanging each bag on a hook under the chalk or marker tray of your board.

Hanging clothes-drying rack. Suspend the plastic rack from the ceiling and use clothespins to display student work. In Jamie Boxler's fourth-grade classroom, students hang their work-in-progress on the rack.

A novel way to display students' work

Mini–garbage bins. Busy classrooms often have an array of snippets on the tables and floors. Several teachers we know place mini–garbage bins (available at discount stores) strategically around the room. This keeps students from having to walk across the room with their hands full of snippets, leaving a paper trail in their wake.

Plastic crates. Turn these on their sides and stack to create inexpensive shelves. They can hold books, student supplies, manipulatives, and so on.

Storing classroom materials in milk crates

Plastic milk jug. Cut a slit about 1" from the bottom of a clean half-gallon jug. This becomes a yarn dispenser. Push the yarn through the slit and pull the starter end out the mouth of the jug. Tie a pair of scissors to the handle, where it will be handy for students to cut off the desired amount.

Using a milk jug as a yarn dispenser

Plastic storage sleeves (for slides or baseball cards). Use these to organize letter cards for making words. Print several copies of letter cards and sort them into each of the plastic sections. These sleeves also work for organizing word cards. Store these in individual notebooks or folders.

Organizing letter cards with plastic sleeves

Shoe-storage bag. Hang a shoe-storage bag over a closet door to organize small items such as paper clips, pencils, erasers, and envelopes. These bags work well for both student and teacher supplies. Post one at your writing center to serve as a mailbox or a message center for students.

Student desks or tables. Leave names posted on each desk or table all year long. This is helpful

Transforming a shoe storage bag into an art supply holder

for substitutes and guest teachers. Cheryl Rocco writes her fourth-grade students' names directly on their desks with a permanent marker and cleans them off with nail-polish remover at the end of the year.

Wallpaper water tray or plastic windowsill planter. Store sentence strips in these trays. Suzi keeps two trays, one for blank strips and the other for printed strips to be used in the pocket chart. You can find these trays in any home-improvement center with the wallpaper supplies, or in the garden shop.

Storage for sentence strips

Work folders. Create student work folders to house ongoing projects. Fold a 12"x18" piece of construction paper in half lengthwise (the "hotdog" fold). Fold another piece in half to make a 9"x12" folder (the "hamburger" fold). Sandwich the 6"x18" paper over the bottom half of the 9"x12" paper to create four pockets. Label the pockets: to be done, unfinished, needs revision, and completed (or similar words). See Table 7 below for an example of the completed work folder.

Outside of work folder:

Completed	(Student's Name) **To Be Done**

Inside of work folder:

Unfinished	**Needs Revision**

TABLE 7

Although using any, or even all, of these organizers will not magically transform you and your students into organization wizards, they will help. Organization does not come naturally to many of us. It takes commitment — and not only from you.

When I was teaching third grade, I created a "when you finish early" bookshelf full of activities the children could take to their seat to practice if they chose. We discussed responsibility and organization several times, but one day, it seemed as if no one remembered. When the students left for the day, the shelf was a *mess!* As I walked over to the shelf and prepared to clean, I stopped myself and thought, "There are 29 of them and one of me, and they need to see this mess." Instead of cleaning, I found some yellow "caution" tape and made an "X" over the shelf. The next day when the students arrived, I told them about the mess and let them know the shelf was closed. After two days with the tape still in place, two students asked me if they could clean the shelf. I removed the tape and everything was returned to its proper place. —Suzi

If we constantly clean up after our students, they do not learn responsibility and we end up spending a lot of our personal time cleaning. Our goal is not for you to never help clean. What works best, in our experience, is to clean and organize *with* our students, not *for* them. The goal is to make students part of the process to create a more functional learning environment.

CHAPTER 5

Finding a Place for Everything

Walk into any school before parent conference night and you're likely to see teachers tidying up. Peek into a classroom before a scheduled observation by an administrator and you'll probably find the teacher cleaning or at least getting extraneous things out of sight.

> What do you do when company comes to visit? Without a doubt, most of us tidy up our space. I admit there have been times when I've shoved dirty dishes in the oven just to get them out of sight! I realize that this last-minute panic made extra work for me. By the time I got back to them, I actually found myself weighing the benefits of throwing them away, buying new dishes, and starting over. But while I scraped the food off, I reminded myself not to let myself do that again. —Susan

Most of us at one time or another have hidden things away in cabinets or drawers. Most of us have stressed out just thinking about our piles of paper, folders, and materials. Hiding our mess or making neat piles gets us through emergencies, but we actually create more work for ourselves with these kinds of short-term fixes. Instead, we can choose to bite the bullet, design a place for all the miscellaneous clutter we've hidden away, and commit ourselves to finally getting organized.

Organizing Yourself

Everyone creates clutter in their own way. In your work area, for instance, what is begging for your attention? Your desk? A counter? A shelf? The trick is to choose one starting point where you will focus — a small, manageable area like a desk drawer, one pile of papers, or a small countertop. Make a commitment to work on this one space until it's finished. The benefits far outweigh the short amount of time you invest. You will feel better about the space and yourself. And you'll be able to work smarter — not harder.

An out-of-control cabinet

A Place for Everything for Teaching

Whatever you choose as a focal point, you need to decide on a place for everything that you want to keep there. If it is your desktop, for example, identify where you will keep your lesson plans, teacher manuals, student work, and so on. At this point, you are not actually moving anything around, simply planning.

Next, designate places for the things that accumulate around your room or that you collect regularly. You might decide to use a couple of paper trays to collect homework, notes from parents, and other signed papers in the morning. You could also designate a tray for papers that are ready to be returned to students. You will need a place where lunch money can be collected. The task is to think about your room and where to most conveniently keep and store things.

It is not uncommon for me to have to search for keys to my classroom, house, or car. Whether at home or at school, I find that I misplace them regularly. As I began to think about a place for everything, I designated a place on my desk at school where I would keep my keys. I quickly learned that my method works only when I return them to that place each time they are used. Making myself do that takes extra effort sometimes, but it is well worth it. I *know* they will always be there when I need them. —Susan

Everything in Its Place for Teaching

Designating a place for everything saves a remarkable amount of time. Once you identify where things belong, you are ready to put everything in its place. Start by going through the papers and materials in your focus area. Sort these things into three categories: keep in this area, relocate to another area, and give away or throw away.

Keep in this area. Keep in your focus area *only* what belongs there. Each item must have a designated space. When in doubt about whether something belongs in the focus area, try asking yourself three questions:

A successfully organized closet

When will I need it? How will I use it? Is this the best place for it? If you answer "no" or "I don't know" to any of these questions, consider relocating the item to another area.

Relocate to another area. When you have finished sorting every item in your focus area, you will have a "relocate to another area" pile. Identify the materials you have a designated space for in your classroom. For example, a box of paper clips goes with all the other boxes of paper clips. Thematic unit materials belong together. Fight the urge to shove all this into a drawer, and put these items where they belong.

Once you have put items into their designated spaces and patted yourself on the back, you need to evaluate anything left in your "relocate" pile. Do you need to create a space for it? Is it worth saving? How do you plan to use it? Let the answers to these questions guide your decisions about where to put each item. This is an appropriate time for deciding to transfer items from the "relocate" pile to the "give away/throw away" pile.

Spring cleaning

Give away/throw away. New teachers and staff members are usually grateful to receive things that can help them get started. Consider giving away your surplus items. When second-grade teacher Megan Cawley began teaching, she started out in a newly created unit with no teaching supplies. Her team went through their supplies and gave Megan many of the things that they had accumulated through the years. It was a win-win situation: Megan was grateful to have some basic teaching materials on hand, and her team welcomed the extra space in their closets.

After you have given away what you can, grit your teeth and throw the rest away. This is probably one of the most difficult things for teachers to do, but as Nike's popular advertising slogan says, "Just Do It!" You will thank yourself later.

A neat, efficient classroom

You have organized your focus area! Sit back and enjoy your accomplishment, and think about how this newly organized space makes you feel. Now is the ideal time to make the commitment to yourself to keep it that way. You have just completed the first step to getting yourself organized. Your next step is to repeat the process with a new focus area, and then another. We suggest that you give yourself permission to work slowly but steadily through this process until your classroom is so organized you barely recognize it.

The Bottomless Tote Bag

As you are getting your classroom spaces organized, you may also want to consider other areas that accumulate teacher clutter. How many teachers do you know who carry home a tote bag? We both acknowledge carrying ours home regularly.

We also admit to rarely opening them at night. In fact, neither of us could quite recall what exactly was in our tote bags. While it's loaded with good intentions (as well as just plain "stuff"), an untouched tote bag can also cause frustration and guilt. The tote bag is no different from those piles we accumulate at school. It, too, needs to be organized and useful.

Take a look at your own tote bag and ask yourself, "Why do I have it?" We suggest that you empty it and sort its contents into the same three piles you used in your focus area. If you cannot part with it altogether, you can experiment by leaving it at school for a few nights. Then ask yourself if you were lost without it. Or, take your tote bag home only once a week or once every other week, with one or two jobs or projects in it. Whatever you decide to do with your tote bag, occasionally give yourself permission to go home and leave school at school.

Getting Students Organized

While you get yourself more organized, you will also want to help your students be more organized. With everyone working together, the organizational structure of your classroom is bound to be more efficient, and helping students learn to become organized is one of the most valuable lessons you can teach them. Later in school and in life, whatever they do, they will do better if they know how to organize. In fact, we can't think of one job or life role that does not require some organizational skills.

Some teachers believe that an organized classroom stifles student creativity and that structure discourages critical thinking. On the contrary, we find that creativity and critical thinking *require* a great deal of organization. As Lucy Calkins notes in *The Art of Teaching Writing*: "The most creative environments in our society are...the predictable and consistent ones — the scholar's library, the researcher's laboratory, the artist's studio. Each of these environments is deliberately kept predictable and simple because the work at hand and the changing interactions around that work are so unpredictable and complex." We can start to create a classroom community that fosters creativity and complex thinking by helping students get organized.

A Place for Everything for Learning

Just as we need a place for everything in our work environment, so do our students — for instance, easily accessible, designated areas for storing their materials or supplies, and cubbies or desks free of excessive clutter. It is enormously helpful to designate places for each kind of item students need for learning. For most students this includes a variety of school supplies such as pencils, paper, markers, glue, scissors, and so on.

Teachers consider school supplies either community property or individual property. Some teachers collect all school supplies at the beginning of the year and designate them community property that students can use as needed. For example, if each student brings in a pack of ten pencils, a teacher might give only two pencils to each student to begin the year and store the others in a central location. As students need a new pencil, they can draw one from this community supply. Judi Blessee, a kindergarten teacher, organizes her community supplies into shower caddies. Each table of four to six students shares one caddy filled with pencils, scissors, glue, and crayons.

Materials that qualify as individual property generally carry one student's name and get stored in a school box or cubbie for use only by that student.

My students bring supplies from a list I send home during the first week of school. As community supplies such as tissues, markers, and glue bottles arrive, I write "Thanks (student's name)!" on the box with a permanent marker. This helps my students to remember and thank the contributors as we use their supplies throughout the year. They also bring some personal supplies such as crayons, pencils, paper, and folders. I label and store half of these in my closet until midyear. At that time, I give each student a fresh set of learning tools. —Suzi

Everything in Its Place for Learning

Organizing the classroom and keeping it organized are processes that teacher and students share. We can make time for students to organize their workspace with our help. Since this is their personal space, they need to learn how to maintain it. One way to start is to have the students empty out the contents of their desks and sort the items into four piles: to go home, stay at school, keep in my desk, and throw away.

Go home. Students should take their "go home" pile straight to their backpack or cubby to take home that day. Discuss with them the idea that anything left longer than a brief period — say, two days — will go in the trash.

Stay at school. Each "stay at school" item needs to be put in its designated place in the classroom. Students may need help with this step.

Keep in my desk. First-grade teacher Brenda Bunker makes a lesson out of organizing desks. For example, she might give explicit instructions for how and where to store materials in the desk. As students put things away, there is an opportunity to practice directional, comparison, and spatial skills. Students could put items back in their desks in any of the following ways:

- Cardinal directions: "Place your math book on the northwest corner of your desk."
- Left and right: "Put your math book on the left side and your science book on the right."
- Largest to smallest: "Stack your largest folder on the bottom. Continue until you have stacked the smallest item on top."
- Alphabetical order: "Organize your books alphabetically by their titles."

- Capacity: "Stack your books with the heaviest on the bottom, then the next heaviest, and end with the lightest on top."
- Measurement: "Place the book that is about one foot long on the bottom of the stack." And so on.

Throw away. Students need to throw away all scraps of paper and other unnecessary items. From time to time, they need reminding to throw away small pencil and crayon nubs.

Some students may not have individual desks, but they can still help with organization. When my kindergarten students organized their crayons, I often did a quick check to see if they knew their colors. I would have everyone dump their crayons on the table and place them back into their cup as I called out the color names. For example, "Please hold up your red crayon. Who does not have a red crayon? Please put your red crayon into the cup." As I glanced around the room, I could see who knew their colors and who needed the help of their neighbors. I continued until all the crayons were back in the cup. We accomplished two goals in the process: The crayons were organized, and I made a quick assessment of color recognition.

Later in the year the students and I organized crayons using new skills. For example, I might ask the students to hold up the crayon that rhymes with "bed" or to hold them up in order of the colors of the rainbow. The students had fun thinking about my clues and getting organized at the same time. And I was able to help them get organized as well as complete an informal assessment. —Suzi

---

The Bottomless Backpack

It's amazing how much stuff students can cram in their backpacks. Many of their backpacks actually resemble small suitcases, although most elementary-school students don't require the large backpacks older students need for carrying home heavy books. We find many students have several months' worth of papers, projects, and school information forms stuffed in their backpacks. Few students empty their backpacks at home every night, or even every week. It's worth taking time regularly to help them organize and maintain their packs.

For example, students can talk about what backpacks are really designed for: to move materials and supplies from one location to another. As with their desks, they can empty their backpacks and sort their finds into three piles: leave at home, return to school, and throw away. Here's your chance to remind students that they are responsible for taking papers that are sent home out of their backpacks at night and giving them to an adult. These are "leave at home" items that should not return to school. Students could store materials that they are to return to school in a folder or binder.

Storing backpacks during the day in a crowded classroom also presents a challenge. Where space is an issue, we have found that two laundry baskets work well for storage. Some teachers buy large storage bins with lids to house backpacks. This keeps them out of sight, but easily accessible.

Maintaining Organization

As you and your students continue to organize the classroom environment, remind yourself to label, label, label! Clearly labeled storage areas, shelves, and bins let everyone know what belongs there. Labels are critical for students when they are working in other learning spaces in the classroom. A label, or a picture and a label, make it clear that in this classroom there is a place for everything, and everything is in its place.

In my K/first-grade classroom, I took photographs of shelves and learning spaces at the beginning of the year. I posted each picture in its space to remind my students not only what belongs in the space, but also how the space should look at the end of each day. This was a simple way to share the responsibility of classroom organization with my students. —Susan

The tough truth is that organization cannot happen only once in a while. In the classroom, it's an ongoing, daily process for both you and your students. The happy news is that as you focus on problem areas and get them organized, your environment will make your learning community more creative and productive.

Taking five or ten minutes at the end of every day for you and your students to be sure that classroom jobs are completed, to check personal workspace, and to prepare for the next day can accomplish organizational wonders. The checklist below in Table 8 helps use that time efficiently.

At the End of the Day

Student: Did I...	Teacher: Did I...
Check my desk or workspace?	Check my desk or workspace?
Write down my homework assignment?	Prepare my lesson plans?
Prepare my supplies for tomorrow?	Gather supplies I will need to teach tomorrow?
Complete my classroom job?	Complete my schoolwide jobs/responsibilities?
Help check the room?	Organize any focus areas?
Put only the things I need in my backpack, including any papers I need?	Put only the things I need in my tote bag, including papers to grade?

TABLE 8

CHAPTER 6

Organizing for When You're Absent

"Structure means the students can carry on without you," according to Harry Wong and Rosemary Wong in *How to Be an Effective Teacher the First Days of School*. We agree. A well-organized, structured classroom will be able to function in your absence under the charge of a substitute teacher. But to ensure that it can, the substitute will need clear, detailed plans. When you are away from the classroom, the students' day should continue almost as if you were there.

In this chapter, we offer two suggestions to organize for your absence from school: a theme-in-a-day lesson plan and a substitute-information folder. Taking the time to prepare these early in the year will save you on those days when you won't be at school — especially when you wake up in the morning not feeling well and you have only 30 minutes to get your plans to school.

Creating Theme-in-a-Day Lesson Plans

Several teachers we know create "theme-in-a-day" envelopes for a substitute. They select a mini-theme for the day, such as pets. Students spend the day reading and gathering information on that theme. Everything they do will focus on the day's topic. With this type of plan in place, teachers find that students manage to learn even in their absence.

Theme-in-a-Day Lesson Plan

Today's Theme: _____

Our Lunch Time:
Specials:
Recess:
Students who are pulled out and time(s):

Read Aloud
Book Title: _____

Read the book with the students. Discuss the book after you read using some of the following questions:

- What did the book make you think about?
- How did you feel when_____?
- Did the book make you remember anything?

Shared Reading
Book Title: _____

Gather students on the floor. Make sure every student can see the text that you are reading. For younger students, use a pointer.

1. Book Walk: Discuss cover and title page. Let students predict what the book might be about. Then slowly turn pages as you discuss pictures and print together with students. Some questions to use during the book walk:

   - What do you notice?
   - What do you think will happen? (fiction book only)
   - What might you learn from this book? (nonfiction book)

2. Read the book. As you read, invite students to join in with you where appropriate.

3. If appropriate, reread the book and include students on special dialogue, rhymes, motions, etc.

4. Student Response: Give each student a piece of paper. Fold the paper into four sections. In the first box, ask students to illustrate the book cover and title. In the next box, they should draw and write about their favorite part of the book. In the third box, they can illustrate what the book makes them think, feel, or remember. In the fourth part, they will evaluate the book. Ask students to note who else might like this book and why.

Writer's Workshop

Write today's theme on the board. Ask students to brainstorm a list of words that relate to this topic. Add these to the board. Give each student a piece of writing paper. They will write the teacher a letter telling what they know about today's theme and what they have learned. Remind them that a letter begins with a greeting and has a closing.

Math — Story Problems

Conduct a brief discussion about today's theme. Ask students to refer to the list they generated during writing workshop. Review some simple story problems. Students will work with a partner to create a word problem using a person or animal from today's theme. After each pair has created a problem, they can share it with another pair.

If you have additional time, use the math flash cards to practice our current math facts.

Theme Time (Science or Social Studies)
Thematic Poem Title:_____

Share the poem with students. Discuss how it connects to the day's theme. Give each student an individual copy of the poem. Practice reading the poem several times together.

Hand out a 12" x 18" piece of construction paper to each student. Have students fold the paper in half and glue the poem inside. They can illustrate a cover and inside picture that goes along with the poem. As they finish, have them practice reading the poem to a friend.

Suggested Theme-in-a-Day Topics

All About Me	Families	Pets
Animals	Farm Animals	Plants
Ants	Fish	Rainforest
Apples	Forests	Recycling
Arctic	Friends	School
Author Study	Frogs	Sea Life
Bears	Future	Seasons
Careers	Holidays	Space
Clouds	Insects	Sports
Community	Nursery Rhymes	Transportation
Deserts	Ocean	Water
Dinosaurs	Our State	Worms
Fairy Tales/Folk Tales	Past	

Building a Substitute-Information Folder

Take time at the beginning of the year to write out specific procedures for how everything gets done in your room in your absence. Write the instructions as if they would be read by someone who has never been in a classroom before. We recommend from experience that you be *very* specific. An example of a completed substitute information packet follows. You should add any other considerations specific to your class or school when designing your own.

Substitute Information Packet

Teacher Name: S. Thomas
Room Number: 401
Grade: Third

Table of Contents

1. My Class List
Paste your class list on this page. Update as necessary.

2. Before-School Procedures
Note any special things that need to be done before students arrive.

3. After Students Arrive — Morning Routine and Morning Work
Write down exactly what students do when they arrive.

4. Morning Paperwork
Note attendance and lunch count procedures.

5. Emergency Procedures
Write down evacuation plan and note any special instructions.

6. My Daily Schedule
Copy your daily schedule here. Remember to include entrance and exit routines.

7. Students Who Leave the Classroom
Note any students who may leave your classroom during the day. Be sure to include times and how they are transported.

8. Instructional Materials
Write down where to find teacher's guides and/or instructional materials.

9. Lesson Plans for the Day

Insert your own lesson plans here — be very specific.

10. Procedure for Behavior Problems

Copy the school-wide discipline plan and/or your classroom plan here.

11. If You Have Questions

Note helpful students and staff on this page.

12. Dismissal Procedures

Include information about classroom clean up as well as actual dismissal routines.

13. How Do I Get Home?

Include a list of how each student goes home. Update as necessary.

Sample of a Completed Packet

1. My Class List

Mrs. Thomas's Third Grade

Brianna A.	Daniel D.	Noah M.
Christie A.	Carolyn F.	Aaron N.
David A.	Madison G.	Matthew N.
Ernie B.	Peyton G.	Juanita P.
Katie B.	Wesley G.	Nolan P.
Seauwn B.	Eric H.	Nikki S.
Carrsyn C.	Tony H.	Angela T.
Mitchell C.	Bonnie J.	Gregory W.
Ronnie C.	Danny L.	Jordan W.
Chase D.	Miranda M.	

2. Before-School Procedures

Student Desks/Chairs. Students remove their chairs from the desktops as they arrive in the classroom. They should put all materials and supplies needed for the day in their desks.

Computers. Turn the two computers on using the switch under the computer table. This switch turns on both the computer and the printer. Students may use the computers as they finish their work or during center time only.

Television. Turn the TV on to channel 6 when you get into the classroom. The morning news will come on just after the second bell. All students are expected to watch the news.

Papers/Morning Work. Morning work is in the basket behind my desk. If they choose not to read or write in their journals, students will come pick up today's work after they sharpen their pencils and put things away.

Other. Mr. Johnson is in the room next door. If you need any help preparing the room for the day, he is available to answer your questions. The students are very familiar with their daily routine. Just remind them that they need to do the same things they do when I am there.

3. After Students Arrive

Morning Routine
Students arrive at this time: 7:45 am
Students are tardy at this time: 7:55 am

When students arrive, they should

1. Hang up their backpacks and coats on the hooks.
2. Sharpen two pencils for today's work.
3. Return homework to the "In-box" located on the small file cabinet by my desk.

4. Put lunch money in an envelope and sign up on today's lunch menu.

5. Put their daily agenda folders on the corner of their desks.

6. Read books or write in their journals until the late bell rings.

Morning Work

1. Students can read books or write in their journals during the morning work time.

2. They may complete any unfinished work in their desks.

3. If they do not want to do any of the above tasks, then they may choose a morning work paper from the basket behind my desk.

4. Morning Paperwork

Attendance cards/books. Attendance cards should be in this substitute packet. If they are not, then you will find them in my mailbox in the office.

Attendance Procedure. The attendance helper's name is on the classroom job chart located by the calendar. The daily attendance helper can go through the cards during the morning announcements. You will need to initial any cards of absent students. The attendance helper will put the envelope out for the office to pick up later in the morning. If a student is tardy, mark the card with a "T" and note the time he/she arrived.

Lunch Money/Count. As students arrive, they will put any lunch money for the day in an envelope. After the morning news, ask the Lunch Helper to tally up the number of lunches and fill out the lunchroom order for our class. Attach this order to the money collection envelope. The Messengers can deliver these items to the cafeteria by 9:00am. Note: If you would like to order an adult lunch or salad, you must write it on this form.

5. Emergency Procedures

Evacuation Maps. Evacuation maps are posted by each exit door and are in the Emergency Evacuation folder by the main entrance.

Signals used in our school.

- Continuous ring – Fire alarm. Evacuate the building via the main route unless otherwise instructed.
- Three Long blasts – Weather alert. Listen for instructions via the intercom system.
- Two short blasts – Lockdown. See instructions below.

Accountability Procedures. Any time you evacuate the building, take the emergency folder located on the wall by the main classroom exit. You will find a class list in that folder. Once you are at the evacuation site, take attendance. Note any students missing on the small blue form. An adult will be around to take the attendance counts from you

Lockdown Procedures (if applicable). During lockdowns, we lock the classroom doors and cover the window with the small black strip of paper in the Emergency Folder (located by the main exit). Keep students calm and continue working unless instructed otherwise. If asked to "take cover," turn off lights and ask students to sit or lie on the floor under their desks. Continue this until the "all clear" is given.

6. My Daily Schedule

7:45 – 7:55	Students arrive and prepare for the day.
7:55 – 8:10	Morning news and announcements. (TV Channel 6)
8:10 – 8:30	Morning Meeting and Calendar Math activities (students in circle on the area rug).
8:30 – 9:15	Writing Workshop
9:15 – 10:15	Guided Reading, Literature Groups, Independent Work, and Literacy Centers
10:15 – 10:45	Computer Lab

10:45– 11:10   Shared Reading in the Content Areas
11:10 – 12:10   Math
12:15 – 12:45   Lunch
12:45 – 1:00   Recess
1:00 – 1:45   Science and Social Studies
1:50   Pack up and Dismissal

7. Students Who Leave the Classroom

Special Classes
Bonnie – Mr. Jones 9:15
Danny – Mrs. Spear 10:10
Gregory – Mrs. Hudson 10:10

Medicine
Carolyn and Noah go
after lunch to the
clinic for medicine.

Tutoring
Juanita (T and Th) with Mr. Allen
Nolan (M and W) with Mrs. Alonso

Other

8. Instructional Materials

Subject	Location
Calendar Math Materials	Table by the rocking chair.
Writing Workshop	Student writing folders located in the crate under the writing center.
Guided Reading/ Independent Work	Guided Reading books are located in three baskets behind the small-group guided-reading table. Independent work is located in the work pocket of this packet.
Science/Social Studies Shared Reading	On the easel next to the rocking chair. Students may sit on the floor during this time.
Math	Teacher's guide on the bookshelf labeled "Teacher's Guides" behind my desk. Manipulatives on the back counter.

9. Lesson Plans for the Day

Insert your lesson plans here.

Additional work. Additional work is located on the counter behind my desk. It is labeled "Additional Work" and may be used if necessary.

10. Procedure for Behavior Problems

Upon violation of a school or classroom rule:

1. Student is given a warning in class.
2. Student is given a "time-out" in the classroom.
3. Student is given a "time out" in another teacher's classroom. Note is written to the parent.
4. Phone call home. (Note: This is to be done by the classroom teacher ONLY.)
5. Student is sent to the office for a conference with an administrator.

11. If You Have Questions

Helpful students

- Carrsyn
- Daniel
- Brianna
- David

Helpful teachers

- Mrs. Summers (Room 400)
- Mrs. Abshire (Room 403)
- Mr. Johnson (405)

Office help

- Mrs. Ippolito (Secretary)
- Mrs. Foster (Secretary)
- Mrs. Williams (Nurse)

12. Dismissal Procedures

Clean-up Procedures

1. Students should write down their homework assignments in their work folders.
2. They should clean up their workspaces (including the floor).
3. They should retrieve backpacks and coats.
4. Have trash monitors check classroom floor.
5. Students should sit quietly and wait until they are asked to go to the door.

Student responsibilities before dismissal

All classroom jobs should be completed before students are dismissed. This includes plants and pets. Students must straighten up the inside of their desks and pack up any materials they will need for homework.

Teacher responsibilities before students leave

Make sure homework is written on the board so students can copy it in their agenda books. Check to see where students go for dismissal. Make sure all classroom jobs are done for the day. Ask students to stack chairs on their desks before leaving for the day.

Teacher responsibilities during dismissal

Put students in a line in the following order: bus students, car riders, after-school care, and walkers. Walk students to each location and dismiss the appropriate students.

Teacher responsibilities after dismissal

Make sure all computers and equipment are turned off. Stack any remaining chairs. Turn off the lights before leaving.

13. How do I get home?

Bus	Parent Pick-up
Brianna	Ronnie
Matthew	Gregory
Aaron	Mitchell
Katie	Chase
David	Peyton
Eric	Tony
Seauwn	Miranda
Bonnie	Noah
Danny	

Walk/Ride Bike	After-school Care
Carolyn	Angela
Christie	Jordan
Carrsyn	Wesley
Ernie	Nikki
Nikki	
Juanita	
Madison	
Mitchell	
Daniel	
Nolan	

Bibliography and Resources

Allington, R.L., & Cunningham, P.M. 1999. *Classrooms that Work: They Can All Read and Write.* New York: Longman.

Fisher, Bobbi. 1998. *Joyful Learning in Kindergarten.* Rev. ed. Portsmouth, NH: Heinemann.

_____. 1995. *Thinking and Learning Together: Curriculum and Community in a Primary Classroom.* Portsmouth, NH: Heinemann.

Fountas, Irene C., and Gay Su Pinnell. 1996. *Guided Reading: Good First Teaching for All Children.* Portsmouth, NH: Heinemann.

Gardner, Howard, 1983. *Frames of Mind: Theory of Multiple Intelligences.* New York: Basic Books, Inc.

Harwayne, Shelley, 2000. *Lifetime Guarantees.* Portsmouth, NH: Heinemann.

_____. 1999. *Going Public: Priorities and Practices at the Manhattan New School.* Portsmouth, NH: Heinemann.

_____. 2000. "Top Ten Bulletin Boards that Teach." *Teaching K-8 Magazine.*

Healy, J. 1990. *Endangered Minds: Why Children Don't Think and What We Can Do About It*. New York: Simon & Schuster.

Kovalik, Susan, 1994. *Integrated Thematic Instruction: The Model*. Washington, DC: Susan Kovalik and Associates.

Routman, Regie. 2000. *Conversations, Strategies for Teaching, Learning and Evaluating*. Portsmouth, NH: Heinemann.

Wong, Harry & Rosemary Tipi Wong. 1988. *How To Be An Effective Teacher The First Days of School*. Mountain View, CA: Harry K. Wong Publications.

About the Authors

Susan Nations is a literacy resource teacher for grades K-5 at Gocio Elementary School in Sarasota, Florida. She is also a national literacy coach, consultant, and speaker, and has presented at many state and national conferences. She is the co-author, with Mellissa Alonso, of *Primary Literacy Centers: Making Reading and Writing STICK!* (Maupin House, 2001).

Suzi Boyett is a literacy consultant for Lebanon Community Schools in Lebanon, Indiana. She previously taught

The authors — Suzi Boyett and Susan Nations

kindergarten and second grade at Gocio Elementary School in Sarasota, Florida, and received her degree from Indiana State University.

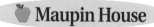